❝❝ THERE ARE NO CLEVER WORDS HERE, NO TRICKERY. THERE ARE NO PROMISES OF REDEMPTION OR DIVINE FORGIVENESS; JUST THE QUIET LAST WORDS OF A MAN WHO HAS LIVED HONOURABLY. IN TODAY'S WORLD OF SELFISHNESS AND EXCESS, THOSE WORDS CARRY A REVERBERATION THAT WILL TOUCH EVERY READER.

— Carlie Lee, *Penfriends UK*

❝❝ THIS IS A GENTLE STORY THAT SPEAKS OF LIFE AND THE LITTLE THINGS THAT MAKE A BIG DIFFERENCE. THE STORY IS WRITTEN WITH GREAT LOVE AND TENDERNESS THAT IS RARELY SEEN. THIS IS A QUICK READ AND WOULD MAKE A NICE GIFT FOR LIFE CHANGING EVENTS.

— Sabrina Sumsion, *Premier Book Reviews*

❝❝ THERE ARE SOME WISE INSIGHTS TO THE MEANING OF LIFE, AND OTHER KEY POINTS THAT AFFECT THE QUALITY OF THE LIFE THAT ONE CHOOSES TO LIVE. A WORTHY LEGACY IS A GOOD READ AND IT IS HIGHLY RECOMMENDED.

— Margaret Orford, *Allbooks Review*

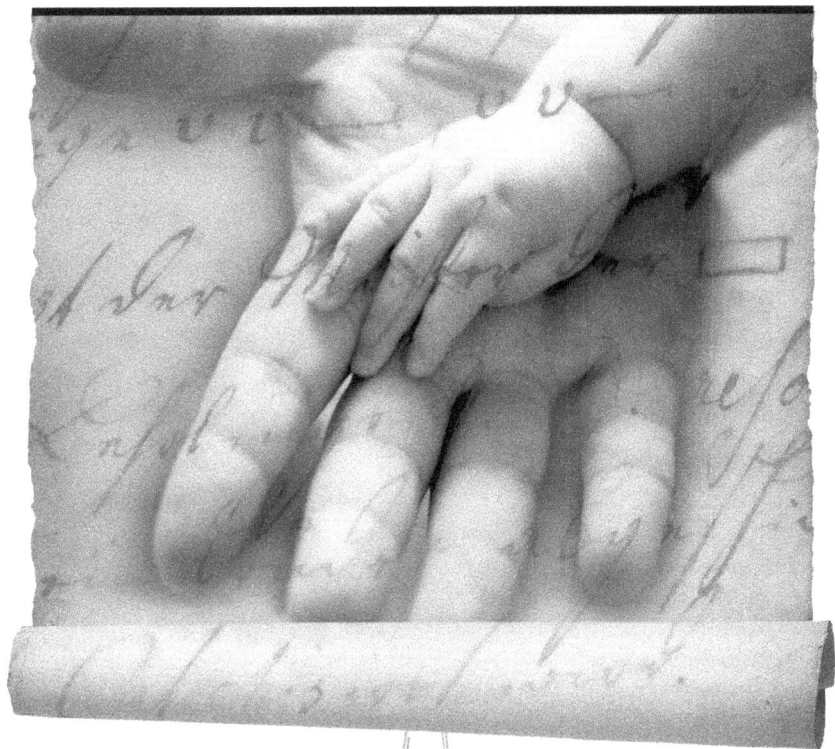

A WORTHY LEGACY

TOMI
AKINYANMI

PUBLISHED in the USA by Tommie Books.
(http://www.Tommiebooks.com)

ISBN: 978-0-615-21116-9 (paperback)
       978-0-615-19619-0 (hardback)

LIBRARY OF CONGRESS CONTROL NUMBER: 2008904623

COVER DESIGN: Cecilia Sorochin (www.sorodesign.com)
BOOK DESIGN: sorodesign
TYPESET: MrsEaves by Emigre

www.aworthylegacy.com
www.tomi-akinyanmi.com

PRINTED IN THE UNITED STATES OF AMERICA

DEDICATED TO MY DAD OMOLADE,
who tried hard to be the very best dad, and
my uncle Oluwadare who was more of a
grandpa to me. You should both know,
you left a worthy legacy.

THOUGHTS ARE LIKE SEEDS,

Born of the fruit of our words.

And like seeds, they could be dispersed.

Your outlet could be your tongue.

As for me, I have chosen the pen.

Tomi Akinyanmi (2008)

Contents

PART I

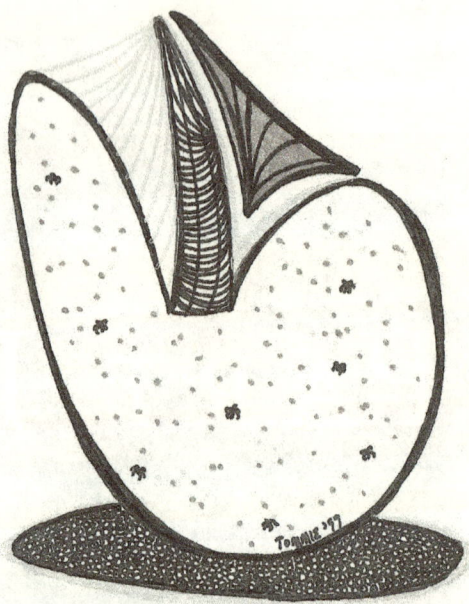

Tommie '17

The Summons

*I*t was a typical November day. The dry and dusty harmattan
wind had started to blow over Nigeria from the Sahara desert,
and the heat from the burning sun was almost unbearable.
I stood at the window of my third-floor office in a twenty-story
building, watching the people below move along the sidewalk, their
petroleum-jellied bodies caked with dust. When the phone rang,
I returned to my desk and picked up the receiver. It was Papa.
I'd dreaded this call since Grandpa became ill a month ago. Even
before he spoke, I knew this was it; his heavy breathing from the
other end of the line gave it all away. For the briefest moment, I
held my breath.

"Grandpa wants everyone in the village," Papa told me.

"I'll be there before nightfall," I replied, and dropped the phone. I felt my heart start to pound, and suddenly it seemed as if my strength had drained away; the thought of Grandpa's impending death was a huge blow. I'd seen him every weekend since he'd taken to his bed, and each time the illness seemed to be getting the better part of him. Yet when Papa told me he believed this was it for him, I wouldn't believe it. I wanted to believe he'd come out of this like he did those times when he had the flu, and the times when he had malaria, but this time Grandpa himself seemed ready to go. He wouldn't eat or drink anything for the past two weeks.

Grandpa was a dear soul. In all my years of life, he had always been caring and loving, but stern when he needed to be. He'd been my babysitter a number of times and doubled as my nanny when Grandma needed to go out. I loved him with all my heart and enjoyed spending time with him. He would often play old songs on his gramophone or tell me stories. Oh, such wonderful stories Grandpa had to tell! I loved the stories of his days in the army, and tales of his students when he was a teacher. I had heard fewer stories of when he was the village representative in the local government council, but I knew that he had been well respected and that his advice had been taken in good faith by the government and the people he represented. Now here I was about to lose him. Life seemed so unfair; I wished he would live on forever.

I cleared my desk and prepared to go. I wanted to spend as much time as possible with Grandpa today; Papa had said he might not live to see the next day. I hurriedly walked out into the afternoon sun and made for the garage. How lucky I felt that the bus I met at the garage was loading for Boluwaji. The next bus heading that way was not due for three hours, and leaving that late would cut into the time I had left to spend with Grandpa. I couldn't bear the thought of that.

I took my seat, feeling melancholy. I closed my eyes and thought of Grandpa. I remembered the nights I had spent with him, Grandma, and his other wives, Mama Bidemi, Iya Ibeji, and Mama Soji. They lived like a big family, something uncommon in the city. When I was but a child, I would snuggle up on Grandpa's lap as he told us stories of his life before he retired to the village.

When I became too big to sit on his lap, some smaller grandchild took my place. It was hard to say which one of us grandchildren was his favorite grandchild because he played with us and disciplined us all the same, but I loved to believe I was his favorite just because he called me his little girl. Of over fifteen grandchildren, I was the first girl after eight boys, and the only one until the sixteenth grandchild was born. So by virtue of my gender and position, I felt I had a rightful hold on his heart.

Memories of my childhood are mingled with days in the city of Lagos, where I lived with my parents, and the village where my grandparents lived. As both places were not too far apart, I got to spend almost as much time in both locations and thus could identify with life in either place, but that did not stop Grandpa from calling me the city girl. For most of my long holidays, Papa and Mama wanted to get me out from under their noses. Mama would pack my bag and have my dad "dump" me in Grandpa's lap. I was always glad to go because Grandpa's home was fun, and I got treats I wouldn't normally get at home. It was therefore no surprise to my parents when I started taking public transport to the village when I came of age.

Today, though, the joy I usually felt when I went to the village was not there. I dreaded going to the village for a cause such as this. I hated to think I was going back to bid my dearest and oldest friend goodbye, and not just for a while, but for the rest of my life. He wouldn't be there to see me married; he wouldn't be there to give my children a hug. I didn't dare imagine how it would feel to watch Grandpa take his last breath, but this was a duty I had to perform. That was the way of my people. Yoruba, the tribe to which my grandpa, my dad, and subsequently I belonged, loved traditions, and why not? Traditions have helped preserve our culture for centuries. Being there by the deathbed to bid the old and dying relative farewell was one such tradition, and the opportunity was considered revered. I consider some of the other traditions either too inundating or obsolete, this was one I had no problem honoring.

The bus jolted over the numerous unavoidable potholes dug on our unpaved road by the pelting drops of the departing raining season, and we were soon there. I knew by the smell in the air, the fresh, unmistakable scent of the farmlands. Slowly I opened my eyes from my reverie and looked around. Outside the window was the familiar sight of cocoa and kola nut trees. Then I saw the huge Iroko tree that marked the boundary of my village. The main settlement was some two kilometers from that point, a distance we covered in minutes. At the entrance of the main settlement was the garage, and that was where passengers disembarked.

I alighted from the bus into the village twilight. The journey hadn't taken long—about two and a half hours in all—but the steaming harmattan sun had my body drenched with sweat. My cramped muscles quickly stretched out and loosened as I prepared for the five-minute walk home. My purse slung over my shoulders, I walked the well-known path to the family house. The familiar sight of mud brick walls and rusty, corrugated iron rooftops welcomed me, but there was an unfamiliar hush over the village as I made my way towards the house; each step I took seemed to grow heavier. I dragged my feet, wanting to prolong the moment of truth - yet longing to see that dear old man. The village was much too small for secrets, and everyone had obviously heard of Grandpa's impending death. The people wore grim faces, and many seemed to be holding back tears. I responded to greetings made almost in a whisper from old friends and familiar faces.

Grandpa was well loved and respected by all. Though he wasn't the oldest man in the village, he was the sage whom both the young and the old sought for advice on almost all aspects of their daily life. He'd resolved a lot of family feuds in his time, reunited husbands and wives who'd sworn never to live together again. He had talked to many runaways, convincing them to go back home, and had escorted many of them as they returned home. Grandpa had had his say in the business circles as well, because he'd tried his hand at business a number of times. His business experiences are another story in itself; I can only say he wasn't cut out to be a businessman. As I hurried through the streets, it dawned on me that the history of the village would be incomplete without him.

From a distance, I could see that the house was unchanged except for a crowd of mourners from the village sitting out front and singing soulful, melancholic songs that sounded very much like death itself. Because there was no crying, I knew he wasn't dead yet.

Anger welled up within me just to see them there. How dare they! I hurried toward the house, suddenly anxious to see Grandpa's face. I wanted that face imprinted in my memory for years to come. I spoke furiously to the mourners and asked them to depart, but instead they wailed all the more, as if to sympathize with me. The sound of my high-pitched voice brought Uncle Soji outside; he held my hand and pulled me into the house. The smell of melon soup welcomed me, and from the background came sounds of pounding. Pounded yam was being made to perfectly complement the melon soup; the meal was ideal in every situation.

I met Papa in the passageway. "E ku ile baa'mi," I said, and knelt down to greet him, for kneeling was the right and proper way for a girl to greet an elder of my tribe. "Sons prostrate, and daughters kneel," I frequently heard from both my parents and my grandparents while I was growing up. Many times, too, I'd seen their secret smile as I knelt to greet an elder in the street, and if it had been otherwise, other parents would have said that I was not properly home trained.

At the sound of my voice, Grandma emerged from Grandpa's room, a finger on her lips signifying silence. I knelt down again to greet her, but this time I was silent in obedience to her. She pulled me up and led me into the courtyard at the back of the house, where a host of cousins, uncles, and aunties, as well as my grandfather's other wives, sat down to eat. Uncle Soji's daughter was pounding the yam; near her was her mother, the typical village wife with her overpowdered face. I knelt to greet the elders in the group and nodded to the children in greeting. Then I followed Grandma into her room, where Mama lay fast asleep on the bed. I dropped my purse on one of the chairs and briefly asked Grandma about Grandpa. She replied with deep lines of worry on her face, and before I could ask other questions, she sneaked out of the room. With nothing else to do, I sat down to eat some of the pounded yam and the melon soup, which Abike brought for me. Afterwards, I joined the others in the courtyard and, like them, waited for the signal from Grandma, who by then had returned to Grandpa's room to stand watch by his bedside, as was her duty, being the first wife.

Grandma came into the courtyard a little after seven o'clock and signaled for Papa as well as his brother and stepbrothers to come. She signaled to the rest of us to wait. They all went into Grandpa's room and emerged some five minutes later, the four men holding the four corners of Grandpa's bed and Grandma holding an extra blanket.

They took the bed into the family room, and Grandma signaled us to follow. The other wives went first, followed by the remaining children and their spouses, then I and the other grandchildren followed (the smallest, just a few months old, was carried in half asleep). When I entered, I noticed the room had been cleared of all furniture so it could contain all the family, just for this meeting. The men set Grandpa's bed down in a corner of the room, and Grandma moved fast to cover his feet with the extra blanket. Then they all moved aside, and there was no veil around the bed; for the first time that day, I saw my beloved Grandpa.

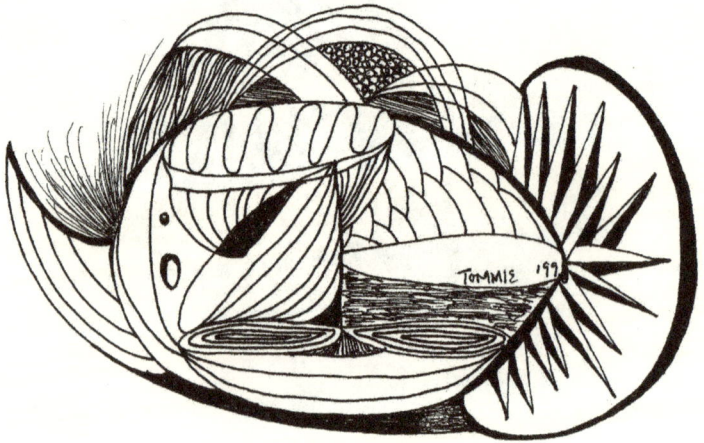

The Gathering

He lay on his bed, fragile and frail, and we all crowded around him to show our love. Children, grandchildren, wives, the family, one and all. With heavy hearts we stood by his bed, willing him to live. Knowing within that his time was spent, with gloomy faces we waited for the dreaded hour. But suddenly he addressed us with a voice loud and clear.

"My dear ones, the hour we await is near at hand. Soon my spirit will vacate its earthly dwelling. But before I leave, there is one duty left for me: that I share among you that which I own."

"I have little property to bequeath, and it's neither silver nor gold. I have no diamonds to leave as inheritances to you. What

I have to give are words, and they are more precious than any other thing I could give to you. I fear that you children, who have sprung forth from my loins might be lost without them when I am no longer here to guide you as I have done from the day you were born. However, I leave these words not only to you, but also to your husbands, wives, and offspring, for they are my children as well. As for my wives, listen to these words, that in the ages to come you may remind these little ones of them. Before I begin to speak, I must ask this favor of every one of you: that you lighten my heart with a smile. For great is the sorrow within my heart to see in your eyes the pain deep within. Don't you know that even I am very sad indeed that I leave you alone on this side of life?"

"I therefore plead with you that you wear a smile just for me, for like the lightning lights up the darkness of the earth in the storm, so does a smile light up a gloomy face; then it extends its glow down into the heart, to lessen the sadness within."

After saying this, he grinned, and it was his famous mischievous grin. It was the first time I had seen it that day, and seeing it once again warmed my heart. It's a grin I'd known for as long as I'd known him, and it always made me smile. Today was no exception, and for a brief moment, I felt some guilt in smiling despite the grimness all around. I tore my eyes from him and took a quick look around the room to see that I wasn't the only one warmed by his grin. There on a couple of faces across the room, I saw the semblance of a smile, and I felt relieved. Grandpa looked us all in the face. Letting his eyes linger on each face, he silently waited until each one forced a smile, then he moved his eyes to the next. When we all had smiled, he nodded his head, and then he began to speak again.

The Last Words of a Dying Man

□, wird alles des Vos.

Ein Heißsat ist Schib

∪ —, ∪ ∪ — gezeichne

Meister der □ ℔ℴ,

... N. N. resolviert

... abgeschickt

... wird. Der

... an der Th..

... dem ersten ℔ℴ

M y dear ones, listen well, both you old ones and you young ones. Through the years, by giving you advice, I have often wiped tears from your faces. Alas, that time will soon be past, for my duty on this side of life is done. What I am about to say will, after I depart, be the guide to lead you through the years. It will also be your shield against those terrors you certainly will face as the years run their toll, until your own purpose is fulfilled. When your purpose in life is fulfilled, then it will be your turn to depart the world. Let your ears, therefore, be opened wide, and your heart be receptive to my words, so that none of these things will be lost to you, lest you have nothing to guide you on your way.

I befriended life while I was yet in the prime of my years;

our friendship yielded many fruits, and these are the words I am about to leave to you. As fruits are eaten that the body might acquire the materials necessary for its growth, these words will indeed give strength to your souls.

> *As we move on in life,*
> *Different phases pass us all,*
> *Wading through different tides.*
> *Joy at times and sadness at others we have,*
> *Yet through it all, this upholds our spirits:*
> *The vision that we pursue.*
> *Different paths each of us must tread,*
> *Though sometimes too, our paths do cross.*
> *Yet we each have a different life to live,*
> *For everyone has a destiny to fulfill.*
> *Thus different dreams lie in each person's heart,*
> *And hopes differ from heart to heart.*
> *Some dreamers die with dreams unfulfilled,*
> *And many who are alive have broken dreams;*
> *Some others come to lose their hope.*

Even then, the living must advance,

For life, indeed, goes on

In as much as we inhale air in this world,

We must bear these thoughts in our heart:

A little while we tarry here,

For life is nothing but a mist,

Here today and gone the next day.

Only if we do to others as we would ourselves today

Can we be remembered for good when our time is done.

Concerning Character

Embrace self-respect as a friend; take him as your companion wherever you go. Then can he lead you away from the wrong paths. For when the storms of life are getting rough, only self-respect can keep you from doing what would put you at the mercy of that foe called disgrace.

Make solitude your sister and find peace in her embrace; therein can your thoughts breed healthy fruits, and then you can attain greatness. Know that solitude often will give you insight as a gift, and when she does, hold on to it dearly, for this is a rare and sacred gift that many seek but never find. Keep it wisely: guard it as best as you can, for if you lose it, you might never find it again.

Let solitude guide your thoughts, for your thoughts make you. I'm sure now you wonder in your hearts, how do thoughts make you? Your thoughts mold and shape you. Thoughts determine where you go and what you do wherever you go. They help build your personality—the kind of person you are—and thus determine what you will make of yourself in life. Note that good thoughts will breed good manners, and bad thoughts will breed otherwise. For this same reason, watch the company you keep - for friends influence what you think. Their words are the fruits from which the seeds of your thoughts are born. Dear ones, I tell you, therefore, that if you want a bright future, then choose your friends with care and pride.

Pride is good when it comes to setting standards for yourself. It is choosing to do what you consider the right things. It is also knowing the difference between what is right and what is wrong for you. However, when you begin to think you are better than others, it is time to check your mind. Always remember that one person is no better than the next. We all are here on this earth because we have a duty to perform. Your duty remains for you and you alone. No one else can fulfill your role; neither can you fulfill another's role. Thus, learn to be humble, and learn to serve. Remember that just as pride soars higher than the peak of the highest mountain, so does humility sink below the depths of the deepest sea. Whatever you do, do it because you believe it to be right and because your conscience allows you to do it, rather than doing it because everyone wants you to. This way, even when it hurts, you will always be able to tell the truth.

Note that if the world praises you, it does not mean that you are right. Receiving accolades is not as important as doing what you know to be right. To do what you know is right and to stand up for it is what the world calls character, and only character can sustain you when all else fails. For this reason, I would admonish that you always look inside yourself. For if you really must know what you are, then must you learn to search for answers within yourself. Deep in your heart, you will always find the truth. Whether you are a good person or a bad one, the answer lies within you. Only in your soul will you not find deceit, and if you never change what you find, that is what you will be forever.

Again, here is something important for you to know: that you will always be unhappy if you try to be like others. However, if you will find who you are and be that, you will have happiness in life. Yet to find happiness then, there are certain principles that you must apply:

> *Let your mind remain a solid core,*
> *Never to be broken*
> *By the changes of time.*
> *Let your heart be like the prickly rose,*
> *Which the best of thieves can never steal.*

> *Let your soul possess*
> *The shining armor of truth,*
> *Which no arrow can ever pierce.*
> *This, I call the recipe for living in peace.*

On Learning from the Past

To find happiness and live in peace is to find balance in the mundane things of life. Discovering balance is no mystery; the secret lies in the recess of your mind. A simple way to unlock that secret within is to give heed to the words I speak now.

Remember the past in all you do,
For this will prevent mistakes.
Yet do not relive the past,
For that will breed destruction.
Rather look to the future,
Wherein lies your vision.
This balance will push you on,
Even when your strength is small.

Never dwell on past victories; rather, strive to make the present worth your while. This will indeed be to your gain. For then can the future be an enticing dream, something you can desire, and thus will you find fulfillment in life. Remember always that

> *Life is a game*
> *We all must play.*
> *Not all will win.*
> *Neither will all lose.*
> *But he who would win,*
> *Must have a lot of courage.*
> *For he will have to bear a lot of pain,*
> *And he will cry a lot of tears.*
> *When he has risen above all these,*
> *He will bear the trophy of success.*

Learn to count your blessings and not your troubles, for what you have, many others do not have. If you can put into good use what you have, you just might be able to call forth what you do not.

Concerning Tough Times

For stormy weathers, I give to you these words:
We are like fishes
In this globe turning round and round.
We jump with the tides and flow with the waves.
Rough or smooth, we cannot relent.
Though our strength fails us,
We must hold on to hope.
To find a haven,
Where neither winds nor storms can move us.
There we will be safe,
And there we can smile
Whenever we recount those bad times past and
All the storms we have waded through.

Existing in this world has much to do with knowing how to struggle. You struggle to get into the world, and you have to struggle to survive. Hence,

Don't you give up when the wind is strong.

Don't give up because the storm is rough.

Don't give up when it seems there is no way out.

Always keep before you, your dream.

Strive to attain the goal

With truth prevailing.

Let sincerity, faith and perseverance be your watchwords.

Continue with diligence to fight.

I assure you that someday, somehow, you will overcome.

On Using Our Initiative

Know this: that you needn't wait for others to try out something new in which you believe. Be the very first at anything you can, and do not let frustrations or defeats hinder you; only then will you have a sense of accomplishment.

Note that frustration and hurts are often a result of expectations not met or fulfilled; thus build no expectations too big that you would be hurt. All the same, you should also remember that if you have no expectations or dreams, you will not progress in life, for there will be nothing to drive you on. For this reason, dare to envision yourself in a place higher than where you are right now, and work towards it. Only if your eyes are set on a goal can you move towards it.

It is true that nobody but you is responsible for your failure, yet where you have failed, you can still succeed if only you will swallow your pride, retrace your steps, and search for the things that you overlooked the last time, no matter how little they might be. Check out those things that you had probably taken for granted as well; these more often than not are the sources of failure. Therefore, if you fail, do not let it bother you; rather, think of it as a chance to make amends. Start again and try another way, but more than anything, whenever you fail, never fear to retry.

It is said that there is no such thing as bad conditions, only bad feelings. Indeed, whatever the condition, our feelings determine how we see it for this reason:

Search out the beauties in our world,
That they might bring your heart some peace.
In the midst of a raging storm.
When hope seems lost,
And life seems forlorn,
Look for beauty in the setting sun
As well as in the crescent moon,
And your faith may be renewed.

Remember that the wilted flower drops to the ground bearing seeds in it. Thus

When clouds of gloom gather,

And the darkness grows so thick

That you cannot see beyond your nose,

Look to the things that are all around.

And in them, you will see

That other side of life,

Which brings to your mind

The promise of a brighter day.

About Fears

Here is something about fear that you should know: often in life, you will come to face what you dread the most. Either of two things could happen. You can face it with courage, conquer it, and then begin to wonder why you ever feared it. Or you can cower in fright before your dread. If you cower, believe me, it won't stop until it turns you into a wreck. For this reason, I would tell you never to run away from your problems. Learn to face and conquer them, knowing that the problems from which you flee today will gain more strength, and will one day gain enough to come back and destroy you.

A Recipe for Happiness

Many who have happiness take it for granted, and when it is gone, will go into the dark places to search for it, ignorant that it never can be found in the grime. While the soul wants for love, happiness can never be found, and if happiness is lacking in the heart, then the soul will find no peace.

Alas, love is so hard to find, yet we all must seek for it. Only we must also not forget that the path of love—real, true love—never runs smooth, and like true friendship, true love would remain unscathed when it passes through the fire. However, do not be dismayed when I mention fire. Indeed, the two most important tests of true love are quarrels and absence. It is also important for you to know that love in the sense of the word is much more than roses, chocolates, and gifts. It surpasses all lusts. It's all about understanding and sharing. It's about forgiving and putting behind you the other's wrongs. Love is a foundation, without which, a home is doomed.

Love is like a seed:
It takes trust and a lot of care to grow.
Like a growing seed in the soil
Needing water and weeding to attain maturity,
Love must be tenderly nurtured,
Lest it be choked with thorns.
Only when it is carefully tended
Can it grow with firmly grounded roots,
Never to be uprooted by the winds.
Then will it blossom with flowers bright.

To crown all that I speak on love, I would tell you this, and you always must bear it in mind, that for you to love someone else, you must first love yourself. He who would be happy, therefore, must learn to love himself, yet he must also learn to put others before himself.

It is indeed true that loved ones will often fail you. Yet you must learn not to hate, but to give even those who have brought you pain, all the love you have within your heart. However, when you give to anyone, whether it is your heart or gifts, give not because you expect or want something in return—be it gratitude or gift—lest your heart be disappointed. Men never do remember to give, and when they do, never give to you what you expect. Some will condemn when you would expect them to praise you, and some will show ingratitude when you expect them to be thankful. For this reason, you must learn to give to others for the sake of giving.

Learn to share your troubles, for nobody knows the inner you, and people can only give a helping hand when they know what troubles you. However, in sharing your troubles, you have need for care, because not all who smile at you are your friend. Indeed, true friends are discovered, not made, yet you won't know the difference until there is a storm. False friends are bound to betray, and true friends will forever stay by you. Even in all these, remember that a day will come when some friend you know today will go away from you, not for anything other than the fact that your paths are each defined; and once the purpose for your friendship in this part of life is attained, each person must go their own way. Even then, you can remain as friends over time if you both understand that purpose for which you met. All the same, you must be wary of even those you know and call your friend, for he who knows you best has the power to hurt you more.

Concerning the Nature of Man

It is true there are two sides to the nature of man - the good and the bad. Know that both of these are foes and cannot inhabit the same dwelling; if in us we want the good to prevail, we must put to death the bad.

Never say to yourself, "I can do no wrong," for every man has a weakness within. Try as much as you can to know what your weakness is. Only then are you truly strong. Keep a record of foolish things you have done, and criticize yourself when need be; then you should endeavor to make improvements as you deem fit.

Do not condemn others; try to understand them. When people criticize you, you must check yourself to see if you are guilty as charged, and when you are convinced you are on the right path, just keep right ahead. People criticize when they are jealous as they do when you do wrong. Learn to take criticism in good stride, for it will only help you to improve yourself. To keep yourself in check

and to help you overcome criticisms, I would admonish you to ask
yourself each day:

> *What do people think of me?*
> *What do I think of myself?*
> *What do people see in me?*
> *What do I hide from them?*
> *What do people know about me?*
> *What do I want them to know?*
> *What do people say about me?*
> *What do I want them to say?*
> *If you can honestly answer these,*
> *You will then have found yourself.*

The image you portray truly affects how people would relate
to you. Yet putting off making a decision, while you wait to hear
what others would say, is nothing but foolishness - an absolute
waste of valuable time. Learn to be honest with yourself, and choose
what your heart tells you to do. Choosing to do that when you
make your decisions determines whether you are matured or not.

Hold no grudges; neither should you hate any man. Learn to forgive; only then can you truly love all men. Know that you are your brother's keeper. However, who is your brother? Is it only he who shares the blood with you? No! Your brother is also the lunatic who runs naked in the street and the thief serving time in jail; you must care for each as your brother. With love, admonish everyone who commits a wrong that he may know to mend his ways. Hug him who delights your heart, but never say to one that he is better than the other; take no preference for one over the other – for this will breed envy, and envy breeds murder. Most importantly, you should know that

> *Believing in whom you will,*
> *Trusting whomever you want,*
> *Judging and condemning all you can,*
> *Does not make you the best of men.*

Instead of judging, think each day how you can please someone else. If you can, put a smile of joy on someone's face; you just might be saving a soul from death.

On the Use of Words

Watch what you say, for words have a power of their own; they are the fruits which yield the seeds of our thoughts.

Like the mortar binds the stones in a foundation,
Gentle words bind the thoughts of a troubled mind
And solidify a doubting mind.
Like poisoned arrows rid life,
Bitter words rid the heart of feeling
To turn flesh into stone.
Like venom are the words of betrayal,
And words of envy;
Gently taking root in the mind,
Maturing to destroy the soul.

Thus when you do not know what to say, it is best to keep your mouth shut, for if you force yourself to speak, a whirlwind might erupt that might destroy not only you but others as well.

Watch, think, and speak, all in that order. Never speak of what you have not seen, and never speak before you think; only then are you truly wise.

If anyone comes to speak to you, listen, for only then can you hear what he has to say. You must also listen well, for only the listener can reap the juicy fruits hidden in words spoken by a wise soul. Yet,

If you believe all you're told,
You will be a fool.
If you believe none of what you are told,
You will be more foolish.
Listen and watch,
Even though it may take a while;
Someday you will come to know
What is the truth is and what is a lie.
For the truth will not ever stay hidden.

Concerning Power

Strive not for power for its own sake (that you might rule others and make them bow to your whims), for such desire would strip your mind of reasoning. Its feel would puff the head and rid the heart of life. It breeds hatred, it commits murders, and it destroys the soul. Strive for power so that you may serve others and give to the world the best of yourself.

Again, when you are in a place of esteem, hold this dear within your heart:

> *Every position is for a season.*
> *Do not let it cloud your reasoning,*
> *For such will rid your heart of feelings,*
> *And this will be treason to your mind.*
> *Moreover, it is for a reason.*
> *Thus it will be to your life a failing*
> *If you allow it to destroy your soul*
> *Instead of using it for good.*

In this same stride, keep this in mind: being in power is no excuse for wrongdoing, and never a cause to take bribes. As such I would admonish:

Never take a bribe,
For if you do, you will pay it back.
You might pay it to cure a sickness,
Or to restore damage to your possessions.
You may pay to redeem your name,
Or it may be to something else.
It might not be that same day.
It might not be the next day.
It might even take many years.
But know that you certainly will pay it back someday.

Bear in mind that nothing—and I mean absolutely nothing—lasts forever; that is why we must get the best from every moment for as long as it lasts. Even though the changes may take time, believe me, they surely will come. Though it takes a long time for a hurt to heal, if we give it a chance, it always does. Know that everything has a time all its own; we need only wait for it.

Regarding Time

Time! How it flies! It wouldn't even wait awhile for you to blink an eye, and soon it makes the hurt you feel today a thing of the past. Even if it is joy you feel, with time they become memories in the heart. Little ones, always bear in mind that time won't wait for you, and when you think you have much of it, you will realize how little you really have. Then when the twilight appears, hurrying might not make a difference.

> *Time after time,*
> *Changes take their toll,*
> *Yet when you sit to think of it,*
> *You really can't discern the time.*

Thus quarrel with no man, and leave no time for regret; neither should you think of him who does not please your heart. For this will only be a waste of precious time. Alas, as this second ticks away, you will never see it again. I charge you to make use of the little minutes wisely, for as drops of water gather to make the flood, so do minutes gather to number your days. Only if you can account gainfully for the little moments can you truthfully say you have lived life and done your duty when the end has come. What will be your gain if, when you leave this side of life, nothing shows you have ever been this way?

However, think not of what will happen tomorrow while it is yet today; live the best you can today, for the morrow will take care of itself. Taking one day at a time is the best way to live, and if you want to live life to the fullest, here is what you should try to do:

> *Be content with what you have,*
> *Yet strive for changes.*
> *Enjoy monotony,*
> *Yet endeavor to try out varieties;*
> *It will make your life more interesting.*
> *Take an interest in life,*
> *Yet never take life too seriously.*
> *Enjoy each day while it lasts,*
> *For it might be your last.*

Concerning the Cycle of Life

One day goes, and another comes; thus the days turn into weeks. Weeks turn into months, and then the months become a year. Years combine into an age, and life itself evolves with age. Many sides of life unfold each day. Here is a simple way to look at all that life entails:

Life is like a boomerang:
It's always turning back.
When you do evil,
Nemesis will bring it back again
To knock on your door.
Life is like a cycle,
Going around and around.
When you do good,
Some good will surely come your way.
Life is like the rose:
It blooms and then withers.

You might at the peak of life
Have everything you want.
Yet one day you will die
And leave it all in the world.
In all you do, therefore,
Let your happiness come first.
Satisfy your conscience,
That you owe no man a thing.
But whatever you do,
You must keep this thought in mind:
Life is like a ring;
It's always turning 'round.

On God

Above all, believe that there is a God, even though He is beyond what we can comprehend. Only a perception of Him is what we can get each day in everything that surrounds us: the things we hear; the things we see; and the things we feel in our world. Give unto Him His due respect in worship, for He is not a being like you but one greater than the world, and even life itself.

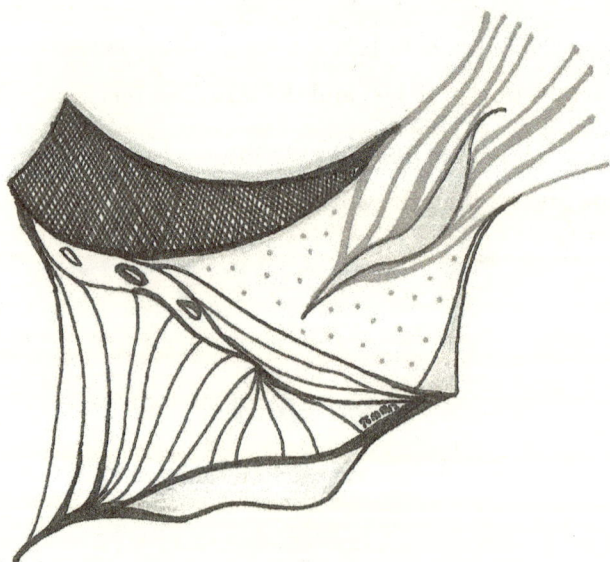

Final Moments

*N*ow we heard him gasp, and then he was quiet for a while. Without a doubt we knew the end was near, and tears began to fall from everyone's eyes. He turned and whispered in Grandma's ear, and she stood up and whispered to Papa. Papa had us all line up in a single file and asked that we go to Grandpa one by one. Then Papa and Grandma went to Grandpa's side and helped him sit up on the bed. Silently we went in a file to grandpa one at a time. With tears in his eyes, dear Grandpa kissed and hugged each one as we came to him. This was his way of bidding us all adieu.

When the very last of us at last moved back from his side, Grandma and Papa took their turn and again laid him on the bed.

Slowly and with obvious effort, he stretched his right hand forth, and, looking towards us, he began to speak again. This time his voice was weak, and growing fainter by the second. "I leave you now with a prayer that these words you've heard from me will never depart from your hearts. May the good Lord bless and keep you all till we meet again on the other side of life." Then his hand went limp, and he left us with a deep breath, a smile frozen forever on his lips.

Immediately, Papa and Uncle Soji covered him up and had everyone leave the room. While the grown men went back in the room where Grandpa's body laid, all the children and us women huddled together in the courtyard and wept in pain. The echoes of our cries reached the village, and we could hear the resounding cries as the village mourned with us. Amid weeping and tears, he was buried the very next day. Grandpa had insisted his body was not to be frozen in the mortuary in a bid to plan an elaborate funeral for him, but that his body be laid to rest as soon as it could be done in a chosen spot within the estate of his home.

PART II

The Gift

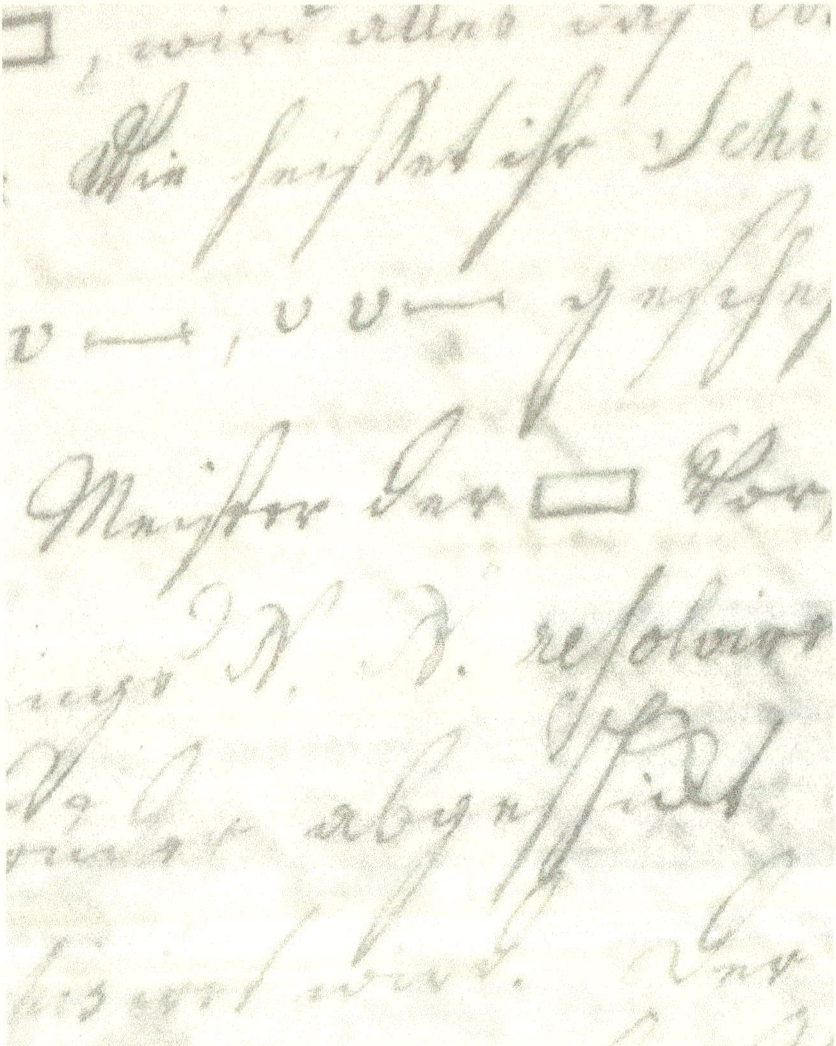

□, wird alles daß vo

Wie heißt ihr Schi

v –, v v – gesch

Meister der □ Ber

...ig N. N. resolvir

...der abgeschickt

...iert wird. Der

...fiegen an der S

...flehet dem ersten St

I t was the anniversary of Grandpa's death. Family and friends gathered for a remembrance service in his honor but only a few members of the family stood beside his grave. Mama Bidemi was dead, and Iya Ibeji, who was sick, had left the village for the city to get better medical attention. Mama Soji was away, in London with her eldest daughter, and of all her offspring, only Uncle Soji came for the ceremony. I had not seen Grandma for the whole year, and it looked as if she had aged a bit; she looked gray and frail as she stood, head bowed, with everyone else.

Many of the others had chosen to stay away, and I couldn't blame them. A lot had changed through the intervening months; bickering, backbiting, and malice had turned the seemingly big, happy family into strangers. Everyone avoided each other like the plague. I looked around the scattered gathering and remembered the last family gathering, at Grandpa's death bed. It was almost unbelievable, the huge disparity between the two. With Grandpa's demise, the thread that had held the fabric of our family in place was gone; there was nothing to hold the different pieces together. Everyone was busy tending his or her pride, creating a wedge to keep them further away. I wondered how anyone could forget how much Grandpa loved to foster peace, and how they could forget his last words.

While each day of the last year I had pondered Grandpa's last words, today was the first time that I had the chance to return to the village since his burial. Standing there, looking at his epitaph, I recalled some past conversations with him. I remembered how, through snippets of seemingly meaningless words, Grandpa had tried to communicate his thoughts on life. I took no notice of those words, as they were meaningless to me at the time. But now when I look back, I understand he'd been trying to prepare me for life, and honestly, though I had had some tough times, in his own way,

Grandpa had succeeded. Through all the unfolding drama of life since the day I bid Grandpa farewell, his last words to us have given me some strength, so that I have been able to face life's struggles not with shock or pain but with a pure sense of calmness.

The epitaph also reminded me of a secret I shared with Grandpa. In the wake of his death, burial, and all the other family matters, it had completely slipped my mind. Grandpa had loved to write, and so I did. The day he found out about my love for writing, he brought out a new notebook and called it our secret journal. There he would write a question and challenge me to think on it and write out my thoughts. How challenging those days were, and how inspiring too. So that it would remain a secret between us both, we had agreed on a place to hide it that was known only to us.

After the memorial was over, I returned with everyone to the family house. I told Papa I would be spending the night with Grandma to keep her company, and this was partly true—I hadn't spent time with her in a while, and everyone else seemed more eager to go back to their lives. The other reason I wanted to stay for the night was to pick up that secret journal. My cousin Ope, daughter of my dad's immediate younger sister, auntie Ibidun, also opted to stay as well, and we chose to share a room.

Once everyone else was gone, Grandma retired to her room to rest, and Ope and I prepared one of the rooms for our stay. Once that was done, Ope also decided to take nap, while I left the room to find the journal. The house looked so deserted, as most of the rooms were uninhabited and locked up. I finally reached Grandpa's old room, and pushed the door open. I turned on the light and looked around the room. It had been kept neat and trim, almost as if he only went out for a walk and would return soon. I went straight to the bed and lifted up the edge of the mattress a little; it was heavier that I remembered. I fumbled around under it a bit and finally found what I sought: our secret journal. I turned around and sat at Grandpa's old writing desk. With shaky hands, I opened it up and turned the pages in anticipation of a final question for me to write, but instead I found that Grandpa had written a message to me, and I began to read …

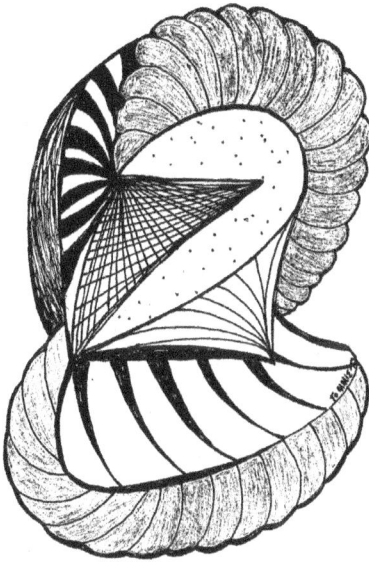

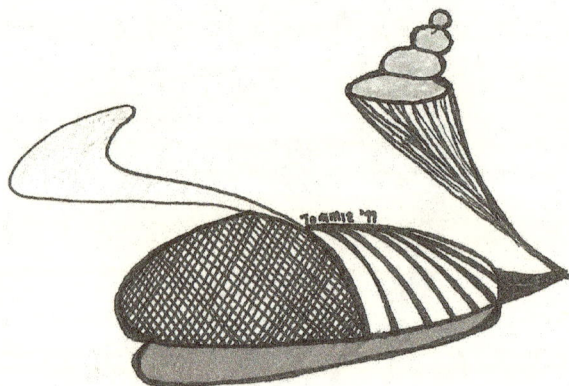

Essence of the Gift

My little girl, life draws close to its ebb. I know of nothing better to challenge you with than with my own thoughts on life. This day I sit to write these thoughts to challenge your thinking everyday from the day you read them. In challenging your thoughts, it is my hope that you would be challenged to live life at the very best like I know you have the power to do. So now I sit and write for you one last time in this secret journal of ours. I sit down to think. I sit down to write. I sit down because life is a story - a story that must be told.

Many questions have troubled my mind since the day I learned to think, and now as life draws to its end, many answers came to my mind; many things unveiled themselves within my very soul tonight, and sleep has eluded me. When the questions rumbled through my mind, their answers immediately came to me as well. So many words flowing through my head - that's why I sit down this day to think and write. I know of no one else to whom I can entrust these words - these thoughts of mine - other than you, my little girl. Therefore, I find our journal, and I sit to write them down just for you - knowing you will know what to do with them.

I have dined with the sage, and I have supped with the fools, yet my encounter with them cannot compare with the truth I am faced with this day. I write the answers as they come to me, unable to keep them to myself, that all may know this truth I've found.

It all began when I thought over my life, which did beg the thought, "What is life?" Then, I heard the echo in my head say, "Life itself is a gift," and I pondered on this.

If life is a gift, it must have been given for a purpose. For if there was no purpose for the gift, the giver would not need to give. Then I heard another echo in my head: "The giver of life gives the gift for a reason."

If there is a reason for life, then what I wondered is its use to the receiver? For a gift without value to him who receives it can be put to no use. As I thought on this, I came to realize life is a gift of worth to him who gave and to him who received.

If humanity agrees that life does have its worth (for I have yet to meet that man who would love to die), why do we spend our life growing and never living, and why do we live and never grow? It seems to me that we often forget that when the novelty of a gift wears off, the gift may not last past that season. As babies outgrow their toys, there indeed comes a time when a gift has fulfilled its purpose, and a time when life's purpose has reached its term. This is why the old must die, for their use of life is fulfilled.

Yet I ask, what use is that gift which is not utilized? For I know that a gift well used would often bring other benefits. As with the happiness children derive from playing with their toys, much joy can come from fulfillment in life. Alas, the benefits of this gift called life can only come to him who would put his gift to good use. To the one who does appreciate life, life will give him many benefits. Thus to leave a legacy for the world to remember you by, know the purpose of your gift and use it as it ought to be used. For,

It is possible to breathe and live,
And then fade away like the morning dew,
If you do not know the value of your gift,
And the purpose for which it was given to you.

When I thought of these things, I realized that visions and dreams are benefits of the gift of life, given to that receiver who discovered the purpose of his gift. Then I asked myself: of what use are these benefits to the receiver of the gift? And it did seem like a tiny voice spoke in my ears, telling me to wait and think. "Yes, think of the clothes you wear," I heard it say. And did I think of this? I thought, and I thought some more. Then, like the light from the morning sun chases the night away, I saw the light of truth disperse my ignorance. Clothes do absorb sweat and rain, but is that the main purpose for wearing the clothes? No indeed, for we wear clothes to cover the nakedness of the body. But clothes do other things for us as well. So also, life as a gift gives that appreciating receiver a chance to dream, as well as the chance to fulfill his dream. Upon this realization, these thoughts came to me:

> *Life holds so much in its grasp,*
> *So much beyond the imaginations of my mind,*
> *Too big a view to behold all at once,*
> *Bigger than I could ever comprehend.*
>
> *New things I see each day.*
> *And I learn new things too.*
> *I once thought there couldn't be more,*
> *But then a surprise came my way.*
>
> *I do understand this now:*
> *It isn't possible for a man to see it all.*
> *Each man will only see*
> *What life has specifically for him.*

Yet if I must, in whatever time I've got,
See all life has meant for me to see,
I must discern the purpose for this gift of mine
While the breath remains in me.

I must learn to live life as I should;
Then I can receive every benefit
That this gift of mine would bring
And then, my purpose is fulfilled.

Also it came to my mind that if I were to keep and hold on to all life gives to me, there would be little room to receive anymore. Yet life will give until the day one dies. What then does one do with the benefits of life that he receives day after day? It was then that I knew why many never have the best that life has to offer them:

If you would receive life's benefits, then you have to give to life. It is only when you have given, that you can receive. For in giving, you create an empty space, leaving room for yourself to receive. That is why you must love others: when you give out the love you have within your heart, then you can appreciate it when you receive love in return.

The human soul is by nature lonely. It finds security and peace in satisfying another soul. That is why a man needs a mate. At this point, I stopped and thought of love, which, I have learned, is a journey of its own. I thought of trips I have made. Not all the roads I have journeyed on have been smooth, yet never have I given up because the road was rough.

The journey may be longer on a road that is rough. Nevertheless, turning back is not an option for him who understands that quitting only takes you back to the starting point. Moreover, if for any reason you divert, the other road may lead elsewhere. Thus,

> A journey is a matter of the mind,
> And what your destination means to you.

This is why you can't give up on love, though the journey to and with it might be rough. The value of true love is beyond any that we can name, and the journey to it is worth its while. I've seen love go wrong, and turn to hate. How much havoc hatred has caused, with murder one of its many offspring. This made me think some more, and I considered murder in all its forms: assassination; homicide; suicide; and abortion. Whatever form it took, I saw no difference among them all. For me, it is and will continue to be denying another (or oneself) of this gift - an irrefutable proof of a lack of appreciation for life. Why we humans are so callous, why some of us are unappreciative of this sacred gift, I will never understand. I wonder why one who cannot discover his purpose must deny another and the world of this beautiful gift. The one who is killed had a purpose for the gift, a purpose that should be fulfilled. But in our insensibility we steal another's hope. In our selfishness we destroy a gift and destroy a purpose too. We not only deny these ones, but we deny the world the residual benefits of the gift and purpose of any man.

I thought about money, a common reason for murder, and I wondered what exactly it is worth.

Money cannot buy you happiness,
Nor can it buy you peace.
Money cannot buy you life,
Nor can it buy you perpetual youth.

Why, then, I ask myself, do men continually struggle to earn more and store more of it? Truly it is not wrong for a man to be comfortable. But when you have too much wealth, of what purpose and good is it to you? The rich man may buy all the cars in the world, yet he can only ride in one at a time. He may have a thousand mansions to his name, but no matter how big his mansions may be, he can only sleep in one of them at a time—and even then, he can only sleep in one room and on a single bed. He can even buy all the clothes he fancies, yet he can only wear one outfit at a time. So how much of the wealth do you really use before you depart the world and leave the rest behind? The rich man's many possessions make him a target for the thieves as well. Why then the daily struggle to amass wealth, if another man may come to take it away from you? But I've also come to understand

All man's struggles
Are more or less to satisfy his soul.
For what he has does not determine his happiness.
The only true happiness would be found deep within,
When the heart is at peace.

At this point I realized that the most important motivation for that entire thing which a man would do, is the reason for its doing. Also, until we can convince ourselves that we have attained what we desired to attain, we thirst for inner peace. Yet,

It is not a matter of what we have,
Neither are a man's achievements a measure of success.

But how do you measure success? First by asking yourself why you do all that you do. When you think of the usefulness to others of what you are doing, then it is easier to know your true aim. Until you can put others first and yourself last of all, there is nothing to be gained from life. Your efforts and struggle to gain wealth is not worth a thing, because the profits they bring to you cannot even guarantee your mind peace. Some men have found peace in helping out another, and some in the sharing of their wealth. Every man has to find his own way to inner peace. However, if you cannot help another man, then you should forget your struggles for riches. Even though a thief may not take what you own, this is something you should ask yourself: how much of it do you really get to use before you depart from the world and leave it all behind? I have also come to know that

> *Hard work does not mean wealth;*
> *Neither does wealth mean class.*
> *Age does not mean wisdom,*
> *And Love does not mean bliss.*

> *Hard work drives vision.*
> *Class comes with confidence.*
> *Wisdom is found in experience,*
> *And love is but a shelter for him who finds it.*
> *Amid all the life storms*
> *A man would wade through,*

Confidence and vision, wisdom and love,
Together pull him through.

Then it came to the foreground amid all these rumbling thoughts: we don't live in a world where all is the way we want it to be or the way it really ought to be. What then can a man do but fit himself into that which he can't choose or change? This, as I have found, is what reality truly means. However being able to know when to face reality and when to stick to fantasies is also a gift in itself. It is another of the benefits of this gift of life, one I've heard called "wisdom"—and we all need wisdom - even in the smallest of things we do each day.

Wisdom comes into play when we sometimes have to go an extra mile. I've learnt that an extra mile sometimes makes the difference. But all the same, I have also seen people who try hard at something, don't succeed, and give it up. Then someone else picks up where the first person left off and makes a success of it. Does that make the first person a failure? No! For it is wisdom to know when to give up and when to persevere. The two cannot substitute for each other; each has its own place.

At this point I thought of patience, another of the benefits of the gift of life. I have heard it said also that the patient dog eats the juiciest bone. But I know that it's not always that the patient dog gets the juiciest bone. The difference between him and the impatient dog is that patience has become a habit for him. This patience has become a virtue so that even when he gets the driest bone, he takes his time eating it and savoring each bite. Thus the impatient dog begins to think that the other dog's bone was better than the one he got.

I thought of the life of a man-child. For a while he has his parents on which to depend, but then comes the time when he has to choose a path all his own, that he might fulfill destiny, the purpose for which he was given life. At this point he must he learn to live, make a home for himself. And in making a home for himself, he must find a wife to embrace. Yet choosing a wife must also be done with care. If he chooses wrongly, he will face much pain. For I have heard hell is better than the home of a woman of fury.

Now, I thought of the woman. Her wisdom is tested in the home of the man with whom she chooses to share her life. No matter how educated she might be, no matter how beautiful her countenance is, no matter her talents, she is judged by her conduct. Her home and children determine her success story, and if she has failed in these, then has she failed in life. But still much depends on the home in which she spent her youth, and that is the role of parents in the world.

Parents are but guardians of a trust of life for generations to come. They show their wards the paths that be and guide them to choosing that which is right. No man can discover another's purpose for him. Everyone has a responsibility to do that for himself. No matter how much parents love a child, they must leave it to him to choose the path he wants to tread. Regardless of how tough it might be, they should stand aside and pray that he will take the right path. This is the very best way for the child to learn.

I have heard some parents label their wards bad and unreliable. I have seen some accuse their children of every sin under the sun. Here is something I heard a while ago: if you point a finger to accuse another, you are pointing the other four to yourself. And I thought on this as well. Indeed, no man exists here in the world as we know it, without a vice. Thus, saying someone cannot be tolerated often means you lack tolerance yourself. As such, an untrained child highlights failure on the part of the parent. If you remember this all the time, you will hesitate to point out another for a vice, and so will parents work hard in that duty life has bestowed.

I also thought in my mind that people who do not know your worth would never learn to appreciate you. Surrounding yourself with such people will help you develop a low self-esteem. The only way to help yourself in life and get the best of all the benefits that this gift called life would bring your way is to surround yourself with people who appreciate you for what you are.

People who celebrate your purpose and life
Would challenge you to reach even for the impossible
And make you believe that you can do it, too.
Though your hands may not touch the sun,

These ones appreciate your trying,
For they see only the good in you.

I thought on this because there have been people who had ideas of what I should be, and there are people who claim to know what I ought to be, yet there are some who have accepted me for who and what I am, and it was the last of these that have, over the years, helped me on to what I have become. It was then that I thought on the words that people speak. They do not make you any less of what you are, or any more, either. What they think does not physically change you, but it oftentimes does affect you on the inside. Should I then take to heart all that people say? No! Praise can make a proud man, and abuse can destroy a weak soul. Once I gained an awareness of this, how people's words can mess with my mind, I made a choice and stuck to it: I do not have to listen to what does me no good, for there are some who speak lies because of their envy.

Now again, I thought about lies. It is true that many people lie to escape from the reality of the truth, yet one lie only breeds another. If you do nothing that should be hidden, then there would be no reason to lie. And if there is no reason to lie, honesty would be an easy virtue, and thus it would be easy for one man to relate to another.

I also thought of yesterday, and I realized that then I dreamt of today.

Today, yesterday is only a memory.
This day, I have to live.
Tomorrow, today will be dead,
Becoming a memory just like the day before.

In the depths of my mind,
I envisioned what the morrow would be like,
And inside me hope was kindled,
Like I know it is for everyone.

I hope to live and see tomorrow,
For while there is a today,
There is a yesterday for sure,

However, the morrow is not assured.

Tomorrow has and always would be,
A hope for mortal man,
Yet in tomorrow lies my hope
To wipe memories of yesterday away.

As a new day conquers the old
And slips back in history itself,
Life should be lived today,
As tomorrow we die.

Yet must we plan life today
As if we live for another century,
For a life that is unplanned
Is a futile journey in itself.

And I also thought of death, the end of all things. Whether rich or poor, kings and slaves in Death's hands are nothing but play things. Death would not spare animals or trees; neither does he spare little or great. When the time has come for Death to strike, neither tears nor begging will hold back his hand; in any place or time, all living eventually succumb to him. This is why each and every man ought to fulfill the purpose for which he received that precious gift called life: that when the end eventually has come, he will have given all he had and thus will go empty into the grave.

My dear girl, now I have written this for you, I feel unburdened and truly free. When at last my body is laid to rest, you can be assured that I have done my part and fulfilled the purpose for my birth. Never forget this, my girl, life is nothing but a gift, and it should be treated as such.

Discerning the Gift

With that, Grandpa ended his thoughts, giving his very last of gifts. By the time I had read it through, the tears were pouring from my eyes. I shut the book, and I wept. I wept because suddenly it all became clear to me: the essence of Grandpa's gifts, and the hidden message behind his words. Those words taught me to look beyond my imaginings and thoughts; they helped me see far beyond the immaturities of my mind. The words taught me to listen for voices beyond my ears— voices from within my soul. Those words brought clarity to my mind, and I began to see things anew.

A Flurry of Thoughts

I used to believe in shades of gray, but really, everything is either black or white. When I learned to think in these terms, I found life was much easier to live. A lot of times, we focus so much on how we want things to be or how it could have been that we lose the joy and benefits the reality of the moment has to offer. No doubt, everyone needs to believe in something good. It is that belief that stimulates action and drives the will to survive. Likewise, everyone needs hope, for without hope there is disillusionment.

When there isn't a focus for the mind, there is a general tendency to take on other people's vision, but when that happens, unhappiness is born. Also, the desire of many individuals to be like somebody well-known is often limiting. If we put into good use what we have available to us and develop our inherent abilities, we often don't end up being that person we dreamed of but, end up being a dream for someone else. Certainly, the health of a man depends on the state of his mind; only when the mind is at peace

is the heart filled with happiness, and this is the beginning of a
healthy soul. Each person needs to find his or her purpose in life
and run with it.

I've come to understand some basic things. When it comes
to fulfilling our dreams, money is not a solution in itself. It is
nothing but a means to an end; if you have no end in mind, the
money is useless when it becomes available to you. Yet if you learn
to save in order to attain your dreams, don't be surprised to learn
that while saving pennies doesn't make you rich, it sure gets you on
your way. In addition, perfect timing is a matter of perspective,
and perspective is a subject of the individual's perception. The
perception of an individual is only as realistic as his involvement.
The less involved we are with any situation, the easier it is to be
unrealistic. All the same, you can never really change a person;
you only change their thoughts. And you don't really change their
thoughts; you merely subdue one thought for another, which means
the subdued thought can resurface at any time if the environment
and situation is right for it. For this reason, it is important that
every man ensure that he is in the right environment with regard to

what he desires to attain. However, being in the right environment to pursue your dreams could come at a cost, for misunderstandings and conflicts could arise even with those people you love if they do not share your vision and dreams.

When misunderstandings arise between two parties and words are unspoken, thoughts and imaginings fill the gap, assumptions take control, and actions are born. While sometimes it is good to clear the air and let everyone speak their minds, sometimes it is just best to let sleeping dogs lie. Understanding that everyone has their own way of doing things and accepting the difference in another person makes for deeper relationships. The manipulator may come in every age and size, and it is possible for an individual to believe that the world revolves around him or her, but it's left to the people around this individual to choose whether to encourage this line of thought or not. This choice makes the difference between acceptance and resentment.

From the moment I read Grandpa's message, my mind seemed to explode with a foray of thoughts, and it seemed as if Grandpa had foreseen this. Suddenly I knew what I had to do. I couldn't keep his message to myself; it was much bigger than I. So I am sharing it with the world. I believe this is what he meant for me to do. Perchance someone like you, reading now, will read these words and gain insight to life anew, seeing things that have escaped your mind until now. Perhaps someone, by reading these humble words of a wise old man, might come to discern purpose and find hope.

As for me, I have no doubt within my heart that if every physical property the dear old man bequeathed were to be lost today, the words and knowledge I've received from him cannot be taken from me. This is the greatest treasure I have received, the very best inheritance of all, an inheritance with no equal: a worthy legacy to bequeath.